BOGNOR REGIS
A Pictorial History

BOGNOR
is the place for Sweethearts.

AGNES RICHARDSON

This postcard, posted in 1911, suggests that holiday romances blossomed on Bognor's sands.

BOGNOR REGIS
A Pictorial History

Vanessa Mills

Phillimore

1995

Published by
PHILLIMORE & CO. LTD.
Shopwyke Manor Barn, Chichester, West Sussex

ISBN 0 85033 975 8

Printed and bound in Great Britain by
BIDDLES LTD.
Guildford, Surrey

To my father, Bryan Ide, who kindled my interest in local history, and to my mother, Patricia, for fanning the flames

List of Illustrations

Frontispiece: 'Bognor is the place for sweethearts', 1911

Acknowledgements

My grateful thanks for the loan of photographic material are due to the following (in alphabetical order):

Barnardo's: 164a.
Bognor Regis Local History Society: 3, 7, 9, 12-14, 16, 17, 20, 21, 24, 28, 115.
Mrs. J. Burton: 97a, 99, 104b.
Mrs. D. Glue: 71, 160b.
Mr. Hackett: 112.
Mr. T. Hawes: 10, 11, 27, 31, 39, 41, 69, 74, 77, 78, 103, 105, 168a-c.
Nyewood Primary School: 83a.
Mrs. S. Olliver: 26, 43, 45, 52, 84 (from Mr. R. Iden's original), 85, 100, 144, 147, 164b, cover photographs.
Mr. N. Reynolds: frontispiece, 4, 15, 23, 25, 29, 30, 32-38, 40, 42, 46-51, 53-57, 59-68, 70, 72, 73, 75a & b, 79-82, 86-96, 97b, 101, 102, 104a, 106-11, 113, 114, 117-33, 138-40, 145a & b, 146b, 148a & b, 149-60a, 161-63, 166, 167a & b, 169.
Mr. K. Scutt: 18.
Mr. A. Steed: 165.

Without the support of all the above, in particular Mr. Norman Reynolds, Mrs. Sylvia Olliver and Mr. Tom Hawes who gave up much of their time on my behalf, this book would not have been possible. My thanks, too, to my mother for mopping my fevered brow and to my family for quietly enduring the wailing and gnashing of teeth as the completion deadline loomed near!

Chapter One
'Changing Tides of Fortune'

The arrival of Sir Richard Hotham at Bognor in 1784 is often heralded as the beginning of life in this sheltered spot, but various communities existed here long before that date.

Many traces of early history have been discovered. Fossilised remains of palm trees and crocodile bones hark back to the tropical Bognor of 70 million years ago. Relics of Bronze-Age settlers have been unearthed—flint tools dating back to 600 B.C. were found in several Bognor locations and at Flansham, while Roman coins were found on the shore between Bognor and Pagham.

Bognor, or 'Bucganora' as it was first recorded in a charter dated A.D. 680 (Cartularium Saxonicum), was home to a small gathering of fishermen and farmers. In medieval times Bognor could boast its own chapel, dedicated to St Bartholomew, but the exact location of this chapel remains a mystery. The chaplain in 1279, Nicholas de Scardevile, was not one of which to boast, however. Along with two others, Nicholas was suspected of murdering William Lewyne of Bognor and was obviously in need of some spiritual guidance himself.

No small hamlet would have been complete in those times without its own set of stocks, regarded as a social necessity. When it was discovered in 1491 that the Bognor stocks were broken, the whole tithing was given just 24 hours to repair them. It was also noted that 'le buttes' were not in good condition either. Used in archery, 'le buttes' were vital since archery practice was at that time a statutory obligation. It could have been that the locals had better things to do? Smuggling was commonplace along the coast, and certainly more profitable than archery practice!

When Sir Richard Hotham stepped into the picture in 1784, Bognor had a rather seedy reputation, consisting as it did 'of only a few huts for fishermen and for persons of the lowest order'. But things were about to change dramatically.

Having decided to abandon an unsuccessful political career, Sir Richard Hotham wholeheartedly embarked on a new project—to create a seaside resort which would outclass both 'vulgar Brighton' and 'stuffy Bath' and in so doing attract royal patronage. Bognor was Hotham's chosen spot.

In just over a year Hotham had amassed 1,600 acres of land in Bognor, South Bersted, Aldwick and Felpham—enough to create his own little kingdom. To hold court, Hotham built himself a miniature palace—Chapel House. Its name was taken from the adjacent chapel, dedicated to St Alban, of which only the clock tower now survives. By the time Sir Richard Hotham died, in 1799, he had invested his £100,000 fortune and there were some forty new buildings to show for it. But when his estate was sold, it realised just £8,300, leaving his next of kin with nothing.

Hotham's ambitious aim had been curtailed by his death; King George III did not feel irresistibly drawn to this embryonic resort and Bognor was never to surpass Brighton or Bath. Nonetheless, Bognor did become a very fashionable rival in the 1790s, with accommodation proving so scarce that visitors were forced to stay at Chichester and travel over. Dukes and duchesses, lords and ladies all came to stay, paying as much as eleven guineas per week to rent a house in the summer. Lady Jersey occupied Dome House throughout August and September 1796, enticing her 'very close friend' the Prince of Wales to visit for several weeks. The future King George IV must have liked what he saw, for he later allowed his only child Princess Charlotte to spend her summers here from 1808 to 1811, staying with her governess as a guest of Mrs. Wilsonn at Dome House.

Her governess, Lady de Clifford, filled the Princess's days with exercise or visits, followed by light study in the evenings. At Dome House, the rooftop dome room became the royal tearoom, from which Charlotte could see the sea and the Downs.

The Princess made many friends during her stay, such as Lord Sudley (later Earl of Arran), Mr. Binstead—whose library just south of the *Norfolk Hotel* regularly battled with the waves—and Dr. Davis, who had written the first Bognor guide in 1807. She took tea with William Hayley at his home, Turret House in Felpham, which inspired the poet to dash off a few lines of verse in honour of the occasion. And when Mr. Richardson, the baker on the corner of Mead Lane, had just finished baking the buns, Charlotte would pop in, sit herself down with a bun and discuss business with him. When she returned to London in October, her maternal grandmother remarked, 'You have grown very fat and very much sunburnt'.

Bognor celebrated all day long with fishermen firing guns in salute and much alcohol imbibed, when Princess Charlotte married Prince Leopold of Saxe-Coburg on 2 May 1816. But sadly tragedy struck on 5 November 1817, when Charlotte and her baby boy died in childbirth. The whole nation was stunned. In Bognor the Jubilee School, set up by Dr. Davis and Mrs. Wilsonn for the education of poor children with Charlotte as its royal patroness, though still being built, was now a memorial to the girl who had won the hearts of Bognor folk.

Such royal approval coupled with the extensive groundwork carried out by Sir Richard Hotham created a wealth of opportunity at Bognor. When the Hotham empire crumbled, speculators had been quick to pick up the pieces. Sea-water bathing was considered good for health and a quiet spot patronised by royalty was just right for investment. But it was easy to get carried away on the wave of excitement, the short-lived Bognor Bank being a prime example.

Through the Bognor Bank, George Isaac Call & Co., shares in 'The Bognor New Town Company' were being offered for sale at £100 each. The company's prospectus outlined their dreams for the town, intending 'to combine utility with ornament'. The proposed houses 'will blend the usual accommodation required for families with the details of architectural beauty. Houses will be unconnected except by light colonnades ... trees and shrubs will be planted ... the rural appearance of the Town and Neighbourhood will be preserved.'

However, such elegant plans and the hint of a railway link along the coast from London via Brighton still failed to draw sufficient support. Even the removal of government trading restrictions with foreign countries nine years after the conclusion of the Napoleonic Wars, and the ensuing feverish property speculation in 1824, failed to convince folk to invest in Bognor.

The company was renamed 'The Bognor & Aldwick Improvement Company' in 1825 and shares were cut to £50. This bid did at last succeed in drawing in a modest number of investors. The money was used to build the New Crescent, later known as Colebrook Terrace and now a car park adjacent to the Regis Centre. But that proved to be the only part of Mr. Call's ambitious plans to materialise. That year both he and the promoter went bankrupt.

During 1824/5 speculators had gone mad, gambling in unsound companies, and then the bubble burst. Financial panic swept the country in 1825, and thousands lost their money as seventy banks broke. Among the casualties was the Bognor Bank. Neighbouring Chichester and Arundel Banks survived but George Isaac Call & Co. passed into the history books.

By the end of the 1820s Bognor had gained a new *Norfolk Hotel* (the previous one had caught fire in 1826), the elegant Rock Gardens nearby and the New Crescent (Colebrook Terrace). Both The Steyne and Waterloo Square were also beginning to take shape. The seed Hotham had planted forty years earlier was continuing to grow.

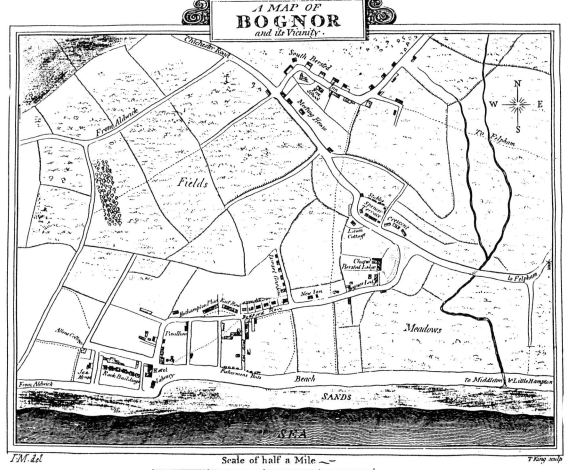

1 Bognor in 1817. Hotham's legacy of impressive buildings formed the backbone of the infant resort. This map was the first town map printed for visitors, measuring 11 ins. by 9 ins. and priced at 6d.

2 Until Hotham's arrival in 1784, Bognor was known only as a resort for smuggling, 'at which time it consisted of a few huts for fishermen and for persons of the lowest order'. Here the fishermen go about their work not far from today's *Royal Norfolk Hotel*.

3 Built in 1792, Hotham Park House was the home of Sir Richard Hotham. At that time it was called Chapel House but later took on the names of Bersted Lodge and Aldwick Manor. The house and grounds became council property in 1946. Threatened with demolition in the late 1960s, the house is now under private management, converted into luxury flats with its essential character remaining intact.

4 The first sea wall protected Bognor's hotel and library, shown here in 1815. The hotel stood near the foot of West Street and burnt down in 1826, to be replaced in 1829 by the present *Royal Norfolk Hotel*. Mr. Binstead's library moved across the road to the Manor House in 1823, to escape the waves.

5 The Rock Gardens, a crescent of 11 houses built in 1804 by Daniel Wonham, which were rented out to visitors at a weekly charge of 11 guineas during the summer, dropping to less than £3 in mid-winter. The houses were demolished in 1980 and modern flats replaced them.

Merchant Taylors' Convalescent Home Bognor

6 East Row, built by Hotham in the 1790s, stood on the north side of Waterloo Square, and comprised six houses offering visitors an uninterrupted view of the sea.

7 South Bersted church was the parish church of all Bognor until 1873. Shown here in 1869, the church dates back to the mid-13th century.

Bersted Church near Bognor

Chapter Two
'Dear Little Bognor'

'Bognor is situated on a dry healthy spot, remarkable for the purity of its air; and those who do not wish to enter the gay and expensive circles of more frequented watering places, will here find a tranquil situation, replete with every convenience for sea bathing, it being the first object of the Proprietor to adopt and promote every plan that can form a respectable and pleasing society.' So announced Sir Richard Hotham's advertisement in the *Sussex Weekly Advertiser* in May 1792, and by the 1850s it appeared that he had been successful in his aim.

Royalty continued to patronise Bognor; Queen Victoria had spent the summer of 1821 (then aged two) at Bognor Lodge and returned again several times for summer visits between 1825 and 1830. 'Dear little Bognor' she later commented affectionately, when receiving the town's congratulations during her Golden Jubilee year of 1887. 'Little' it was, for by 1850 the population still did not exceed 2,000 and entertainment was very limited indeed. But the quietness of the place gave Bognor respectability and, combining pure air and sea bathing, the town became an ideal location for the Victorian family on holiday. The high spot of Bognor's calendar was Goodwood week, when race-goers poured into the town and local traders discovered Christmas came twice a year! Then everything would settle down again to a steady pace.

A ripple of excitement, and some misgiving, ran through the town in 1845 when it seemed that the railway was about to extend to Bognor. The line was proposed to run down to Gloucester Road, but this was not to be, and instead Worthing was linked directly with Chichester. A board announcing 'Bognor Station' was erected at Woodgate and many a visitor on arrival must have wondered just how small a place Bognor really was. Six years later, in 1852, the notice was changed to 'Woodgate, for Bognor'. Neither did anything to shorten the 3½-mile journey into the town itself, which cost the traveller a further shilling on the waiting cart.

When the railway finally did reach out to Bognor in 1864, the town was in celebratory mood—business could only get better!

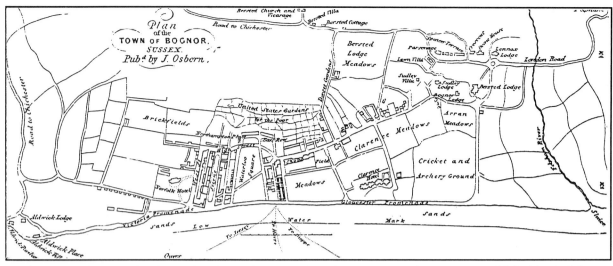

8 This map of Bognor has been taken from *The Visitors' Guide to Bognor and its Vicinity*, published by J. Osborn, *c*.1852. 'The United States Gardens for the Poor' (sometimes called Canada Gardens) shown in the centre of the map were simply allotments and were later replaced by Canada Grove and Crescent Road.

9 Built by Sir Richard Hotham in the 1790s, the elegant terraces of East Row and Hothamton Place were the first to grace Waterloo Square, then called Hothamton Field.

10 The Pavilion, which stood until 1930 on the north-west corner of Waterloo Square. In the 1800s, it was home to Mr. Walters who reputedly invented the gimlet point on screws because he could not abide hammering in his house! The house was demolished *c.*1930 by the owner Harry Humphrey, who hoped to build a cinema on the site. This idea was vetoed by local authorities and Seaview Court now stands in its place.

11 Looking to the west side of Waterloo Square, this view (*c.*1920) shows the row of smart, bow-fronted residences that were built in the 1820s by Daniel Wonham and his son, William, and let to visitors for as much as 11 guineas per week.

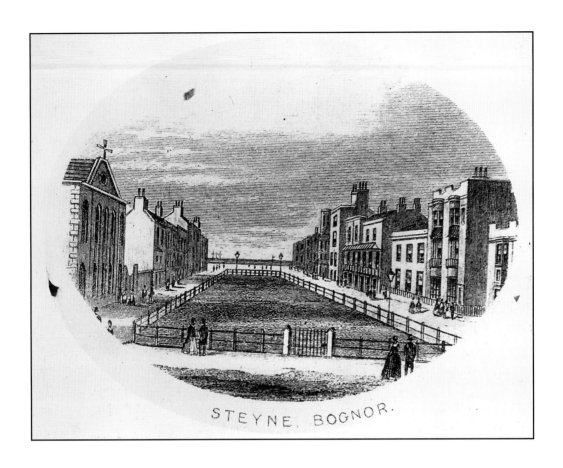

STEYNE. BOGNOR.

Eng by Newman & Co 48 Watling St London

NORFOLK HOTEL.   WEST STREET.   VICTORIA PLACE.

Bognor.

Marine Parade & Rock Buildings, Bognor, Sussex

12 *(above left)* The Steyne, *c.*1850, looking south. On the left stands St John's Chapel, built in 1821 by Daniel Wonham and to which a tower was added in 1833. When Bognor became a parish separate from South Bersted in 1873, St John's became the parish church. It was demolished in 1891 and the stones used to build St John's Terrace in Highfield Road.

13 *(below left)* This mid-Victorian engraving of West Street also shows the *Norfolk Hotel*, which became 'royal' in 1857. The new owner at that time, John Naldrett, included the royal coat of arms in his advertisements and the hotel became known as the *Royal Norfolk Hotel* without any apparent royal link. However, a visit by Emperor Napoleon III in 1872 put that right.

14 *(above)* Marine Parade and the Rock Gardens lining Bognor's west promenade in 1853. Marine Parade was built in the 1840s by Edwin Curtiss, forty years after the appearance of the Rock Gardens. It was here, at the latter, that Sir W.S. Gilbert is reputed to have written much of his successful operetta *The Pirates of Penzance.*

15 High Street—steadily growing as this engraving of the mid-1800s shows. Morris's cheap shoes are being advertised on the corner of Lennox Street and in the distance stands a canopied York House which was to make way for the Arcade in 1902.

Aug. 1872

High St Bognor

16 This view of Bognor's High Street in 1872 shows ever increasing bustle. This may have something to do with a visit by Emperor Napoleon III in the same month (August) in which this scene was published. The Bognor Pebble Establishment on the right would polish up rough pieces of agate for visitors to take home as souvenirs.

SUSSEX HOTEL. ALBERT TERRACE. SUDLEY TERRACE. RUSSELL PLACE.

Bognor

Eng. by Newman & Co. 48 Watling St. London

17 The eastern end of High Street in its infancy. Shown here *c.*1845 are the *Sussex Hotel* (now the *William Hardwicke* public house), Albert Terrace, Sudley Terrace (built in the 1820s) and Russell Place, all still standing today in varying degrees of splendour.

18 Munday's Cottage, September 1868. Part of an old farmhouse dating back to the mid-18th century, it was owned by a cobbler, Mr. Munday. Queen Victoria, as a young girl, is reputed to have purchased her first pair of boots here. Later, it became better known as the Tuck Shop, standing on the north-east corner of Gloucester Road until its demolition in 1968 for road widening.

Chapter Three
'Pier, Print and Prudery'

The arrival of the railway at Bognor acted as a catalyst to the town's development. Within ten years Bognor gained a pier, a police station, its very own newspaper and several new chapels, plus a much needed concrete sea wall. Between 1778 and 1875 it is estimated that as much as 158 yards of shore was claimed back by the sea—if Bognor was to grow, a sea wall was essential.

The pier was opened in May 1865 and consisted of a simple 1,000-ft. jetty with a small kiosk at the shore end. Those wishing to view Bognor from above the waves paid a toll of 1d.—bathchairs were charged 4d.

The police station, a wonderful Sussex flint building, stood at the north end of London Road (then Dorset Gardens), not far from the Water Tower. The latter had but a brief career in the 1880s as the water supply became salty within just five years.

The increasing population of the town led to the creation in 1873 of Bognor as a separate parish from South Bersted. St John's Chapel in The Steyne was no longer considered large enough and plans were made for a new St John's Church to be built in London Road. This was completed in 1882, with the spire finally being added in 1895, three years after the acrimonious demolition of its predecessor.

The *Bognor Observer & Visitors' List* appeared for the first time in May 1872, the creation of Henry Lovett. Just three months later a special copy printed in gold was presented to the town's distinguished visitor, the exiled Emperor Napoleon III, who was staying at the *Royal Norfolk Hotel*. The newspaper was often used by Mr. Lovett as a platform from which to air his views and he would often endeavour to stir Bognor traders into a little more action: 'The peaceful quiet of Bognor is delightful ... but let us beware of becoming too drowsy'. Indeed, his opinion was shared by many visitors. In July 1886 Mrs. Anne Bowman Dodd, an American, commented: 'Bognor was so decorous, so painfully clean, so oppressively self-conscious a prude, that dullness must have been as much a part of its being as were its demure little airs of conventional propriety ...'.

Bognor residents were resisting any change that might 'lower the tone' of Hotham's refined watering place. Change was on its way, though. Speculators were busy planning what to do next. By the end of the Edwardian era, Bognor would be quite different.

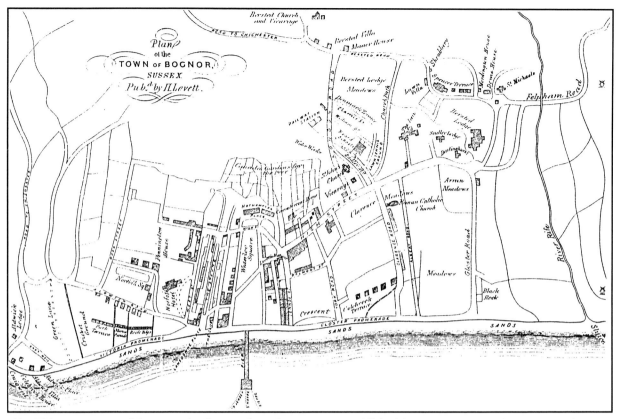

19 This map appeared in *Lovett's Illustrated Guide to Bognor*, published by Henry Lovett, the *Bognor Observer* newspaper editor, in 1882.

20 Bognor's pier was officially opened on 5 May 1865. At that time it was simply an 18-ft. wide jetty extending 1,000-ft. out into the sea. It cost £5,000 to build, but charged only a modest penny to walk its length.

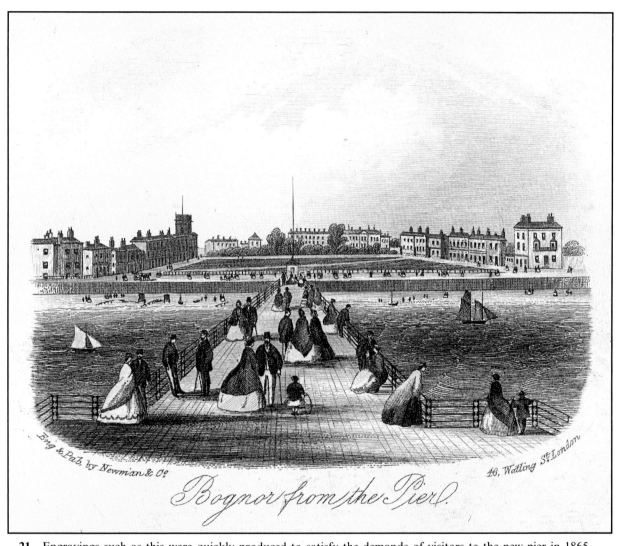

Bognor from the Pier.

Eng. & Pub. by Newman & Co.

48, Watling St London

21 Engravings such as this were quickly produced to satisfy the demands of visitors to the new pier in 1865.

22 This photograph, taken
*c.*1890 from the east side of the
pier, shows bathing machines
and fishing boats working
alongside. On the left, nets are
hung from the wall to dry,
whilst bathing costumes and
towels are stretched across sun-
warmed brickwork.

9 BOGNOR. — Esplanade. Looking East from Pier Gates. — LL.

23 Standing by the entrance gates to the pier, this was the view of Bognor's seafront in early 1909. The Kursaal was still on the drawing board and an open field, nicknamed 'the cabbage patch', stretched between the present *Carlton Hotel* and Colebrook Terrace (now Belmont Street car park). From here Sait's Dairy offered visitors locally-made ice-cream but business was not always brisk.

24 A parade to celebrate the relief of Mafeking in 1900. In the background Mr. N.J. Wilmott has cycles for hire (left of picture).

25 Opened on 4 April 1906 by Princess Alexandra of Teck, the Surrey Women's Convalescent Home received women patients from several Surrey hospitals. The home's regulations in 1912 stated that 'Patients are only received on Thursdays, and may proceed to the Home by any Train, but should arrive at the Home not later than 5 pm'. Also, 'Patients will make themselves useful in such ways as the Matron shall direct'.

26 Cambridge House in Clarence Road, 1916. This was the Children's Convalescent Home for Surrey. The building shown was later demolished in 1929 and a second house built in 1930. The latter made way for a new block of private residential flats in 1982.

27 Regatta Day in Bognor, 1885. A variety of boat races plus ladies' and gentlemen's swimming races were held, with cash prizes of up to £3. A greasy pole contest kept spectators further entertained, until the finale when a mock sea battle was fought and an old fishing boat set alight amidst fireworks.

28 *(above)* The Thespians, led by 'Uncle George' (August Sears) arrived in Bognor in 1897 and stayed. Afternoon and evening performances were given on the sands south of The Steyne and a special children's song and dance competition held every week. Noel Coward won a prize here from 'Uncle George', singing 'Come along with me to the Zoo, dear', in 1904.

29 *(above right)* Another well-loved Bognor entertainer in 1908—the Bognor Clown and his dog, Towzer. Frank Bale paid £1 per annum to rent a pitch on the sands south of the *Royal Hotel*, and would perform with marionettes, play the banjo or guitar, juggle or simply 'clown around'.

30 *(below right)* Tamarisk Walk, west Bognor, at the turn of the century. Note the beach hut belonging to Arthur's Home (now Ashley House).

31 High Street, *c*.1890. The white building on the right, the old regency York House, was surrounded by wooded gardens which later made way in 1902 for the present Arcade.

32 Sudley Terrace, *c*.1905. Built in the 1820s, the terrace had remained residential until Mr. Price set up as an estate agent and auctioneer at no.1, *c*.1900. Then the Coplestone Bakery opened at no.4 in 1903, changing to millinery and blouses in the 1920s under the management of Miss Unwin.

33 Derby House, and Regency villas Valhalla and Manora, in High Street, *c.*1890. Derby House was the home of Bognor's first post office in the 1790s and from here Joseph Ragless and his wife distributed the mail until 1839. Derby House was demolished in 1939 to allow Lyon Street to be widened.

34 The High Street shops (including Long & Strickland shown here) have strung up the bunting in celebration of Queen Victoria's Golden Jubilee in 1887.

35 High Street, *c.*1890. On the right the Congregational church stands at the corner of London Road, then still a residential road called Dorset Gardens. The church was built in 1869, but increasing noise from traffic caused the site to be sold in 1929 to Timothy White Ltd. A new church was built in Linden Road.

36 London Road, looking south, *c.*1900. On the left is Bognor's first Roman Catholic school, the water tower and St John's Church. The landlord of the *Alexandra Tavern*, on the right, also ran the bakery next door. The two premises were merged in 1909.

37 The 2nd V.B. Royal Sussex Regiment, I Company, and Regimental Band, celebrating Queen Victoria's Diamond Jubilee in 1897. This photograph was taken beside St John's Church in London Road, by Mr. W.P. Marsh, a noted local photographer who had successfully exhibited prize-winning pictures of 'Rough Seas' at Crystal Palace four years earlier.

38 T. Walls' hairdressing and shaving saloon in Manor Place, with a sideline as a tobacconist, *c.*1890.

39 The White Tower in Aldwick Road. Built in 1898 by John Cyril Hawes at the age of 21, this same young architect went on to build cathedrals all over the world. The neighbouring *Arlington Hotel* was demolished in the late 1960s when road widening was planned. Luckily the White Tower escaped the same fate and is now a listed building.

40 Claremont House in West Street, built in 1828 as a hotel which became a shop in 1887. This 1915 advertisement shows a smart frontage displaying millinery, fabrics and footwear.

41 The Owers lightship, anchored approximately seven miles to the south-east of Selsey Bill, provided a warning to other vessels since 1788. A foghorn was added almost a hundred years later, probably deafening the 11-man crew, who worked two-month shifts in rota. The ship was replaced in 1973 by a 40-ft. high, 100-ton LANBY—a Large Automatic Navigation Buoy.

42 Strathmore Gardens in Glamis Street, 1893. Harris and Archie (aged two) Gibbs stand in the centre of the picture.

43 *The Railway Hotel*, London Road, was built in the 1860s, but now, 130 years later, it seems to have come to the end of an era.

44 Bersted Street, *c.*1910. On the right is the South Bersted school dating back to the early 19th century and, in the distance, the *Queen Victoria* pub, which became a private residence in 1978.

45 The old *Prince of Wales* inn at South Bersted. The building was believed to date from the 17th century, and in the 1800s was known locally as the Bacon Loft as bacon was smoked up in the roof. It was demolished in 1922 and replaced by the present *Friary Arms*.

46 Ivy Lane, South Bersted, *c*.1900, with its beautiful Sussex flint cottages.

Chapter Four

'Booming Bognor'

The turn of the century was also a turning point for Bognor. Another wave of frenzied activity resulted in new pier buildings, the Kursaal entertainment centre, promenade bandstands, a hospital, cinemas, another church. The pier pavilion, built in 1902 at the southern tip of the jetty, was to entice steamboats to call. The *Worthing Belle* was just one to make a stop here, but problems with the tides meant that the steamers never were able to make Bognor a regular port of call.

Faced with a large repair bill for the pier, the local council decided to sell it off in 1909 for a nominal amount—just 10s. 6d.—to Messrs. Shanley and Carter. These enterprising gentlemen added extensive shore-end buildings, at a cost of almost £30,000, which comprised a theatre, cinema and 12 shops. The investment proved worthwhile.

Whilst workmen were busy on the pier, to the east the Kursaal began to take shape. This 'first class place of entertainment', adding more shops and another theatre to the seafront together with a skating rink, tearoom and Constitutional Club, was completed in 1910 under the watchful eye of William Tate. Mr. Tate had already built an arcade in 1902, leading from the High Street down to the seafront. In fact, it led rather neatly to his Kursaal.

Convalescent homes were springing up rapidly along the seafront, especially to the east, and royal dignitaries would visit from time to time to open such establishments. The town's size now merited a cottage hospital and fund-raising, coupled with the generous donation of Springfield House in Chichester Road by Mr. James Fleming, succeeded in producing the Bognor War Memorial Hospital in 1919. It contained just four wards and eight beds plus an operating theatre upstairs. Benefits from the very first performance at the new Picturedrome cinema in 1919 were donated to this worthy cause.

Mr. Lovett's sleepy Bognor was beginning to wake up.

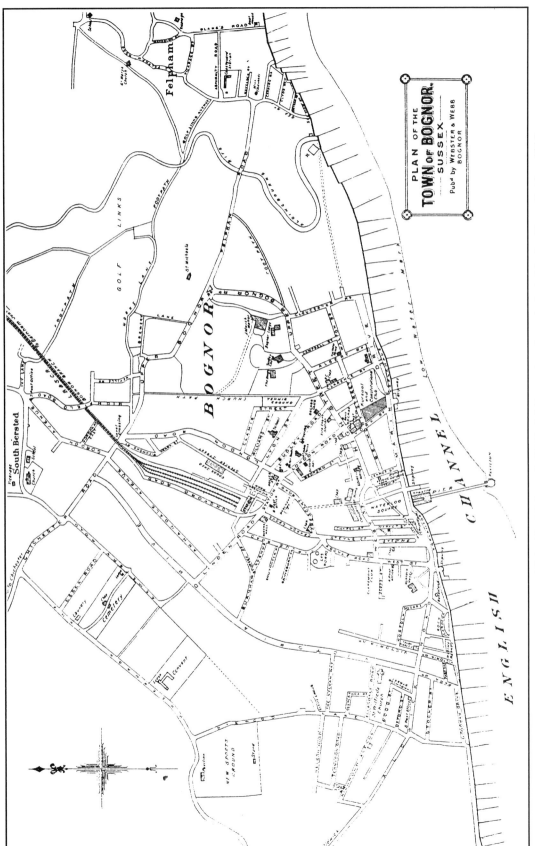

47 This map of Bognor was published by Webster & Webb (of Bognor) and was included in the *Town Guide, c.*1915.

48   The Kursaal under construction in 1910. William Tate was the creator of this ambitious seafront 'palace'. Tate was an energetic entrepreneur whose projects included the Arcade, the Victoria Convalescent Home, residences in Campbell Road, part of Bognor's sea wall and railings. He is also credited with the introduction of electricity to the town.

49   The Kursaal opened in 1910 as 'a first class place of entertainment', encompassing a skating rink, theatre, Constitutional Club, shops and tearoom. Refurbished in 1947, it was renamed the Rex Entertainment Centre. In 1975 the building was demolished and the Regis Centre took its place several years later.

INTERIOR OF THEATRE.   VESTIBULE.

50 Cecil and Eric Pashley land their two-seater Henry Farman biplane on Bognor's beach, 26 May 1913. They gave flying exhibitions and for two guineas would take passengers up for five-minute 'flips'. Their arrival drew large crowds and the shops were reported to be deserted on the day.

51 The town was famous for its postcard views of 'High Seas'. Mr. W.P. Marsh, a local photographer, exhibited a similar scene in a Bond Street (London) window back in the 1890s; such a large crowd gathered to stare in amazement at the view that police were called to clear the obstruction.

52 After receiving an £11,000 estimate for repairs, the local council quickly sold the pier in 1909 for just 10s. 6d. The new owners, Messrs. Shanley and Carter, invested almost £30,000 and added a shore-end building which included a theatre, cinema and 12 shops, shown here being constructed.

53 The promenade, east of the pier, 1909. The fishermen are landing their catches mid-morning (they would have set out at first light) and their tarred prawn and lobster pots line the promenade. In the background stands the Kursaal, as yet unfinished.

54 A dramatic view of a zeppelin flying over Bognor. The first German zeppelins flew to Britain in 1915, Norfolk towns being the first targets to be bombed by these 'humming birds'.

55 The boys of Colebrook House, a private school established in 1885 on the Esplanade. It moved from Colebrook Terrace in the 1930s to the corner of Annandale Avenue, then to Neville Road before finally closing its doors in the early 1960s.

56 *(left)* Pupils from the Eversley School for Girls, in Colebrook Terrace. These 'angels' include Miss Dorothy Cook and a Miss Webb. Daughters from families 'in trade' were welcomed—not true of all educational establishments.

57 *(above)* Colebrook Terrace, built in the 1820s, included the *Royal Clarence Hotel* (run from 1905-28 by Miss Elmslie as a hotel exclusively for children accompanied by their nurses or nannies), the Colebrook House School for Boys and the Eversley School for Girls. The Terrace was demolished in 1947 and ever since has remained a car parking site.

58 *(below)* High Street, *c.*1910. Reynold's, Staley's, Buckle & Clidero, Long & Strickland are amongst those lining the south side, whilst the *Anchor Inn* faces York Road.

59 When royalty came to Bognor, not only were the flags flying but elaborate arches were also constructed for the regal entourage to pass through. This occasion was in 1906 and the High Street arch was in honour of Princess Alexandra of Teck.

GOD BLESS HER ROYAL HIGHNESS

60　Another arch, this time in Station Road. Again the occasion was in 1906 when Princess Alexandra of Teck came to Bognor to open the Surrey Women's Convalescent Home on the seafront.

61 55 High Street, *c.*1910. Mr. Ward sold his handmade cigarettes at London prices (Will's 'Capstan' Navy Cut cigarettes were 10 for 3d.). Next door Lloyds bank looks discreet with its solid door and curtained window. By the 1950s no.55 was a café and Lloyds had moved along to 39 High Street.

62 Leverett & Frye, at 51 High Street, could supply 'tools for all trades', plus much more besides. They also sharpened lawnmowers, decorated houses and fitted gas appliances. At nos. 41 and 43 was Leverett & Frye's grocery shop, selling fish, poultry, game, vegetables, wines, as well as provisions. They had opened for business in the 1890s but were replaced by International Stores by 1919.

63 An advertisement for Reynolds & Co., *c*.1915. The Reynolds business was established in Bognor in 1867 and has expanded considerably since that date. The company is still very much a family concern today, selling a wide range of quality furniture as well as operating a long-established and highly regarded funeral service.

ARTISTIC HOUSE FURNISHING

The Best Selection in the Town

Telegrams:
"REYNOLDS,
AUCTIONEERS,
BOGNOR."

Telephone
No. 182.

Furniture Depository · Inspection Invited

Reynolds & Co.

Complete House Furnishers

27 & 29 High Street
Bognor

**Specially Built Repository
for the Warehousing of
Furniture**
Strong Room for Valuables

ii.

F. W. PEACOCK
Late HARDHAM

Telephone No 49
47 and 60 High Street, BOGNOR

Luncheons
Dinners and
Teas
Provided

Wines,
Bottled Ales
and
Stout

Photo by   Donald Massey

Baker, Cook and Confectioner   3 DIPLOMAS AWARDED

iv.

64 An advertisement, *c*.1915, for Peacock's, the bakery. Here resided a parrot which, when customers entered, would say, 'What the bloody hell do you want?'.

F. HAWKES & SON
9 High Street —
—— BOGNOR

9 HIGH CLASS GROCERIES   F. HAWKES.   PROVISIONS WINES & SPIRITS 9

The Oldest
— Local —

Grocers

Tea Merchants,
. Italian .
Warehousemen,
Provision,
Wine and
. Spirit .
Merchants

Telephone No. 31

The BOGNOR House, Estate and Apartments Agency.

The most reliable information FREE.

ix.

65 Fred Hawkes came from London in 1869 and went into partnership with Mr. Rusbridger. As grocers in those days combined the business with letting apartments, Mr. Rusbridger would await visitors at the railway station, wearing an easily recognisable white top hat.

66 Formerly Mr. Hounsom's library in the 1840s, when printed matter was not the only line on offer—pianos, harps and time pieces were also available for hire. It was here too in 1872 that the *Bognor Observer* newspaper was born. This advertisement, *c.*1915, shows that Webster & Webb now run the library.

67 William Jones' garage in Belmont Street, *c.*1915.

68 A Bognor Urban District Council dustcart, *c.*1900. The council was formed in 1894 and survived until the arrival of Arun District Council in 1974.

69 The wedding of Robert Hawes and Helen Walters at South Bersted church in July 1905. The wedding coach was pulled by Bognor fishermen.

70 Bognor's volunteer fire brigade, established in 1873. They were, left to right—top row: H. Newell, E. Dobbs, A. Norris, F. Ragless, H. Watkins, F. Row, A. Florence, L. Booker; middle row: T. Keywood, (Gardiner) Booker, C. Tate, F. Booker, A.T. Kingsley, P. Hammond, Jessie Ide; bottom row: T. Pipson, Supt. T. Start, W. Keed, Capt. E. Wood, Supt. Harmer, Supt. Keywood Snr., T. Walls.

71 Volunteers enlisting to fight in the First World War, here standing outside the drill hall in Bedford Street.

72 Flooding in Gloucester Road, 1911. The houses on the left were bought up by Butlins, who then made plans to demolish them in 1964. In fact, the houses survived until 1970, after suffering neglect during the intervening years.

73 Argyle Road, *c.*1910—Cavendish and Bassett Roads did not spring up until after 1913. Since the late 1800s this area, called Fairfield, was host to the town's annual July fair, with roundabouts, freakshows and pugilist fights.

74 Taken in 1911, this photograph was snapped from a window of Goodwood House on the north-east corner of The Steyne. On the right is Market Street, then the rear of the Pavilion and, beyond, the tree-lined northern side of Waterloo Square. On the extreme left of the picture is part of Slaney's antique shop (later West Side Merchants and now Seaward Court).

75a Linden Road led from the town to a golf course, which opened in 1892 immediately south-west of the present Victoria Drive/Linden Road roundabout.

75b Linden Avenue was developed from the roundabout through to Hawthorn Road during the 1920/30s and has now been absorbed in name as an extension of Linden Road.

76 The Bognor & Bersted Verion Steam Laundry was started by Miss Lucy Verion in the 1890s and this view shows the ironing in progress upstairs at their Hawthorn Road address. Washing was hung out to dry on long lines running from Hawthorn Road to Town Cross Avenue. After changing hands several times, the laundry finally closed at Hawthorn Road in 1994.

77 Mr. Walters sitting on Big Rock, west Bognor, with grandsons George and John Hawes in 1914. Shrimp nets are ready but a boat might prove more useful!

78 These men are obviously expecting royalty, judging by the arch they have proudly constructed near the foot of Park Road. The black mill on the right was used to grind local rock into Bognor cement—applied to the front of many a local building. By 1910 the mill had become derelict and was demolished that year.

79 Wood Street, west Bognor, in 1909. Houses began to appear here from 1874. The land, which had originally been bought by Sir Richard Hotham, was subsequently owned by the Scott family.

80 Aldwick Road, *c.*1919. Belonging to Edwin Thorp, a chemist, the plot on the right was used by him to grow vegetables. When he sold the land, the Broadway with its mock Tudor gables was duly built in the 1920s.

81 One of the earliest traders in Aldwick Road, Thomas Tregear opened his grocery shop on the north side at the turn of the century. About fifteen years later he also opened an estate agency across the road from his grocery business.

82 The *Victoria Hotel*, built as part of the Victoria Park Estate in the 1880s, survived for just over a century. The *Vicuna Hotel*, the scene of a dramatic rescue in the novel *Wheels of Chance* by H.G. Wells, is thought to have been in reality the *Victoria Hotel*.

83a Nyewood primary school, Richmond Avenue. Built in 1898, it opened on 3 September 1900 to welcome 38 pupils.

83b The class of 1906 at Nyewood school. The school's attendance had swelled to over 105 pupils and that year a stray cow had wandered into the playground, inadvertently knocking down a gatepost whilst being ushered out again! The children are, left to right—top row: Chafer, E. Screach, S. Ide, F. Dench, C. Janman; second row: S. Freeman, M. Pudduck, Froude, C. Ward, Parkinson, K. Ide, B. Lewis; third row: S. Cooke, H. Court, G. Parkinson, M. Clinch, K. Millest, H. Maybey, J. Tansley; fourth row: C. Johnson, B. Allen, Rishman, Pudduck, N. Pudduck, J. Gibbons, A. Goldring, F. Griffen; front row: A. Toye, E. Ide, A. Cooke, J. Taylor, K. Tansley. The school building was demolished in 1976, after pupils had transferred to the 'new' Nyewood in Brent Road in 1975.

ROYAL NAVAL ACADEMY, BOGNOR

VIEW FROM CRICKET FIELD.

FOR NAVY BOYS
Special Preparation for
Examinations and Scholarships.

Special individual Tuition for OSBORNE COLLEGE, AND SCHOLARSHIPS AND ENTRANCE EXAMINATIONS FOR THE PUBLIC SCHOOLS.

Fine Buildings (specially designed), with Large Grounds close to the Sea. Large and well-fitted Gymnasium, Library, Carpenter's Shop, Cubicled Dormitories, Cricket and Football Fields (six acres).

PRINCIPALS—H. W. WHITE, B.A., LONDON, C. G. KEALY, M.A., OXON
xi.

84 *(top left)* Designed by Arthur Smith, the Board school opened in Lyon Street on 9 June 1874, at a cost of £4,500. Initially, 133 boys were enrolled there, 100 of whom had never been to school before. During the school's lifetime, it also temporarily housed the public library and the town's museum collection. It was demolished in 1969.

85 *(above left)* Hambledon Place, which stood in Victoria Drive until the 1980s. Once known as the Courtfield House School for Girls (from only the very best families!), it boasted in 1915 hot water heating throughout and a spacious gymnasium. Later it became a private convalescent home.

86 *(left)* The Royal Naval Academy, for 'navy boys', as this 1915 advertisement states—sons from naval families. Better known now as Streete Court in Victoria Drive.

87 *(above)* Shripney Road, South Bersted, *c.*1905. A far cry from the nearby industrial estate, which was started in 1976, covering some 22 acres, at a cost of £2,500,00.

88 *(right)* Brickley & Co., agents in 1915 for 'the cheapest light on earth', had extensive premises in West Street. The 'Dutch Oven' café now occupies part of the shop.

FULL UP EVERYWHERE AT BOGNOR

89 Bognor was a very popular resort, ever since Hotham's day in the 1790s. Even then accommodation was scarce and seemingly expensive; people were known to stay at Chichester simply because Bognor was 'full up', and then commute daily to take the beneficial sea air and waters. This postcard was sent in 1908.

FROM A GIDDY NIPPER AT BOGNOR.

90 This picture postcard was sent in 1913 'from a giddy nipper at Bognor'.

Chapter Five

'The Royal Seal of Approval'

Another visit by royalty was once again to put Bognor firmly on the map. King George V, still very frail following a life-threatening lung infection, arrived at Craigweil House by motor-ambulance on 9 February 1929. His three-year-old granddaughter, Princess Elizabeth, came to visit, making sand pies in the garden.

Bognor was in a state of feverish excitement as the Prime Minister and the Archbishop of Canterbury both made their way to the King's bedside, and Queen Mary frequently attended local churches and went shopping. When she popped into Woolworth's one Monday, accompanied by Princess Mary and Princess Helena Victoria, the locals, not to mention the store manager and staff, were stunned that royalty should frequent what was deemed 'a working class shop'. An offer of £500 was made by Woolworth's for any photograph taken of Queen Mary's visit but the potential advertising coup never came off and the £500 went unclaimed.

The King was finally declared fit enough to return to Windsor and the royal party left Bognor on 15 May 1929 through a sea of well-wishers lining the route. The local authorities were not slow in writing to the Home Office for recognition and the reward swiftly returned. In a letter dated 1 June 1929 Bognor was informed that the town had His Majesty's permission to add Regis to their name. Sir Richard Hotham would have been very pleased.

During the 1930s the number of shops rapidly increased, with the likes of Burton's and Marks & Spencer opening new doors in London Road. On the seafront Billy Butlin opened his zoo in 1933 and any trace of 'genteel refinement' was gone. Day trippers were pouring into the town; over the August Bank Holiday in 1937, 50,000 visitors arrived. A third-class return rail ticket from London cost 3s. in 1910; by 1937 the fare had increased to 8s. 6d. but this did not deter record-breaking crowds requiring an extra 36 trains to be run to Bognor that Bank Holiday weekend. Bognor Regis was booming.

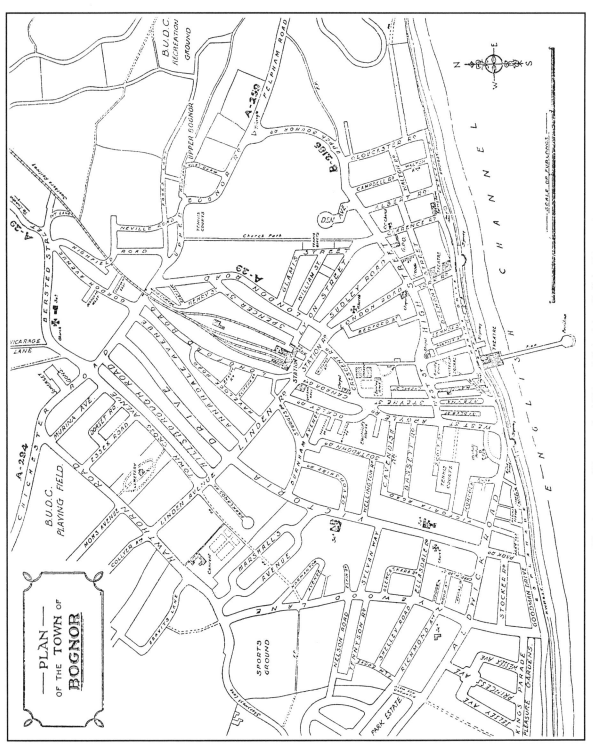

91 A map of Bognor in 1930, published by *Kelly's Directories*.

92 Donkeys on the sands at Bognor in the early 1920s. In the background stand the *Carlton* and *Beaulieu Hotels*, with the Kursaal to the right of the picture.

93 The beach is crammed with holidaymakers enjoying the sunshine in the late 1930s. Billy Butlin opened the Bognor Zoo in 1933, clearly recognised here by the large outcrop of 'mock rock' to the right of the picture.

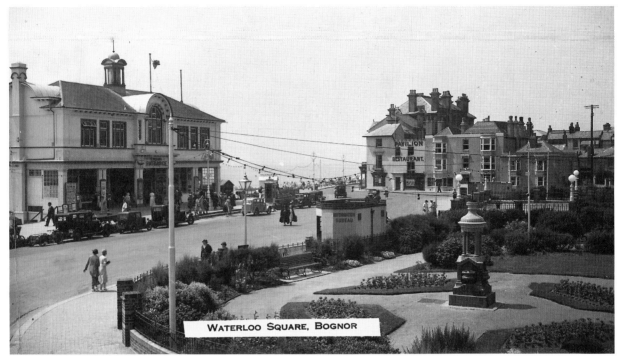

WATERLOO SQUARE, BOGNOR

94 Bognor pier looking across to Queen Victoria's Jubilee fountain. This was erected south of The Steyne in 1897, moved to Waterloo Square, was later dismantled and stored and finally rediscovered and returned to The Steyne in the late 1960s.

95 Holidaymakers are liberally spread over Bognor's sandy beaches in the 1930s. The *Carlton Hotel*'s terrace is in the bottom left corner of the picture.

96 Beach huts and a bathing station lined the east promenade in the mid-1930s.

97a In the Pavilion Gardens they are putting the finishing touches to the new boating pool, which was officially opened on 12 April 1937 by the Marchioness of Cambridge. In the background is a fountain, a rustic bridge and P.I.M.C.O.—Bognor's Co-op store until the early 1960s.

97b The boating pool, shaped in the outline of England and Wales (presumably there was not enough room for Scotland), nestled alongside the Pavilion. Now the area has been turned into a car park, despite strenuous local objection.

PAVILION GARDENS, BOGNOR

98 The fountain, surrounded by a lily pond, once kept the boating pool company. The rustic bridge delighted many children in the 1930s.

99 The flags are flying in Chapel Street for King George VI's coronation in May 1937. The girls standing in the doorway are Doreen and Eileen Marner. These terraced cottages, many home to fishermen over the years, were demolished in 1970 and a health centre built on the site.

100 Once a seaplane assembly shed at Middleton, a lath-and-plaster façade of twin towers was added and the result was the Pavilion, which opened in 1922, just north of Waterloo Square. With capacity for 3,000 people, the Pavilion was used for dances, plays and exhibitions. After a fire in 1948 the Pavilion was demolished in 1949, dashing hopes of reconstruction.

101 Waterloo Square (shown *c.*1937) is still a welcome open space, 200 years after it started life as Hothamton Field. A covenant, designed to protect the unbroken sea view from Sir Richard Hotham's East Row and Hothamton Place, forbade building upon this area, with a penalty of £5,000 per acre should anyone attempt to do so.

WATERLOO SQUARE GARDENS, BOGNOR

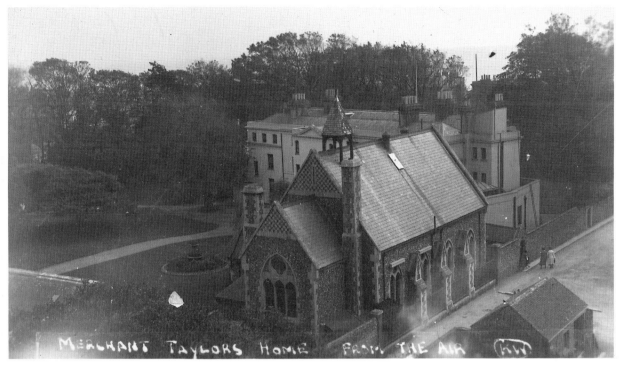

102 Hotham's East Row was bought by the London-based Merchant Taylors' Company in 1870 and used as a convalescent home for its members. It was sold to property developers and demolished in 1955, the chapel shown here meeting the same fate in 1959; now Fitzleet House (a block of flats) occupies the site.

103 The bandstand enclosure at the foot of West Street, *c.*1929. The bandstand was built in 1901 at a cost of £60 and enlarged in 1910. It was later replaced by the Esplanade Theatre, which itself was demolished in 1980.

104a   Marine Park Gardens, opened in 1935.

104b   Building the fountain in Marine Park Gardens, *c.*1935. With his workmate 'Ginger' Denyer, Reg Masters, on the right, completed all the stonework and even built the walls enclosing the Gardens. The two onlookers on the left were gardeners.

105 Bognor High Street in 1929. At this time Bognor Motors, on the left, occupied the old Methodist chapel site. The chapel had originally been built in 1840 and enlarged in 1865. A growing congregation meant that further expansion involved a new church on the north-east corner of Waterloo Square, opening its doors for the first time in 1924.

106 Timothy White's occupied the corner of London Road and High Street for over fifty years. The firm took over the site in 1929 after the Congregational church abandoned the busy spot in favour of a quieter location in Linden Road. This view, dating from the early 1930s, shows the basic electric street lighting inaugurated back in 1913. Long garden frontages remained on the north side of the High Street, hinting at its former residential nature. Nowadays, shops have gobbled up this prime space and glass-plate doors now swing in place of garden gates.

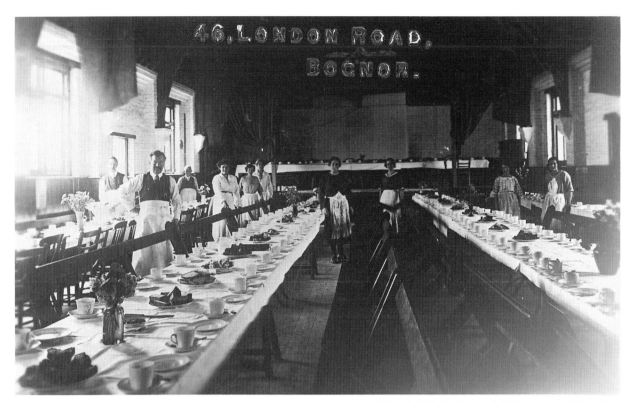

107 St John's Parochial Rooms at 46 London Road, now Macari's café.

108 The water tower in London Road, built in the mid-1870s. Here a 330-ft. bore hole yielded 15,000 gallons of water per day, but in just five years the supply became salty. The tower was then used as offices and finally provided a temporary home for Bognor's public library before its demolition in 1936.

109 Laying the foundation stone at the Bognor Boys' Club in 1938. Prince Henry, Duke of Gloucester (wearing a light suit) officiated, and facing him are Mr. T. Marshall (B.R.U.D.C. chairman), Mr. William Fletcher and Dr. Michael Ayres.

110 Festivities were staged at the Hampshire Avenue recreation ground in celebration of King George V's silver jubilee in 1935. Judging by the van on the left, Antarctic ice-cream was in plentiful supply.

111   The official opening of the William Fletcher School in Westloats Lane, May 1939.

112   The class of 1924 at South Bersted school.

113 Chichester Road, near the *Royal Oak* at North Bersted, 1934.

114 Entitled 'Farm Scene—North Bersted', this postcard view was sent to London in 1938.

115 Crowds gather on 22 May 1929 to witness the laying of the foundation stone for Bognor's new town hall in Belmont Street.

Chapter Six
'Entertainining the Troops'

For the past 150 years Bognor had been busy building. All of a sudden it appeared that a new broom was wanting to sweep clean. Some buildings were at far greater risk from the local authority than they ever were during the Second World War. Colebrook Terrace was one such casualty, demolished in 1947, and the spot has remained a car park site ever since. The Pavilion dance hall was another, still a sore point with those Bognor residents who remember it so well.

Attempting to maintain the town's success as a seaside resort in the face of stiff competition along the coast, the local council wished for a winter garden. Money being tight, a thrifty solution was found: a disused seaplane assembly shed at Middleton was purchased, camouflaged by a lath-and-plaster facade of twin towers, and surrounded by gardens. It cost just £16,500 and opened in the summer of 1922. With capacity for 3,000 people, the Pavilion was used for dances, plays, congresses and exhibitions. Here Bognor heard Albert Sammons, Mark Hambourg, Jack Hylton and his band and George Robey. The Chamber of Trade's town guide of 1926 waxes lyrical: 'The splendid Pavilion floor is a delight to dancing feet, and if you come here on Carnival nights, you will find it difficult to believe you are in an English seaside town ... the illusion that you are not in Paris or Nice will be difficult to dispel'.

During the Second World War the Pavilion was a hot-bed of romance, with Bognor girls encountering Canadian and Norwegian soldiers stationed in the area. Although the Pavilion remained unscathed throughout the War, its days were numbered. On 14 July 1948 the fire brigade was called. In less than an hour the eastern tower had collapsed in flames but the local fire brigade assisted by crews from as far away as Worthing finally managed to control the conflagration. Plans were made to use this chance to improve the building and the council approved a £76,000 reconstruction scheme. To be encased in brick, the façade of the Pavilion would now sport a first-floor restaurant with panoramic views through a semi-circle of windows.

It was estimated that the Pavilion could be reopened after about twelve months and the town waited expectantly. Imagine the shock when the Council did a complete 'u-turn' and invited tenders for demolition. By the end of 1949 the Pavilion was no more than a memory.

South of the *Royal Norfolk Hotel* a new horseshoe-shaped band enclosure had opened on 19 June 1937 at a cost of £4,500. Immediately after the Second World War the band enclosure was granted a roof and finally, in the early 1950s, at an additional cost of £40,000, the enclosure was converted into the Esplanade Theatre.

One of the most enduring shows was that of Eric Ross's 'DAZZLE', playing throughout the summer seasons; Clive Dunn was among the cast of the 1953 show. Every morning, and twice in the afternoons, the Field Puppet Company presented their famous Marionettes from mid-July till September. Constant entertainment was provided.

Nearby, tide and weather permitting, floodlit bathing was organised. Beach games for local children during the summer holidays were also organised on the sands beside the theatre. Another attraction, Hotham Park, was now open to the public, having been bought by the local authorities in 1947.

Bognor was shifting its balance, trying to weigh up what was wanted both by residents and by the lucrative tourist. Not always were the right decisions made.

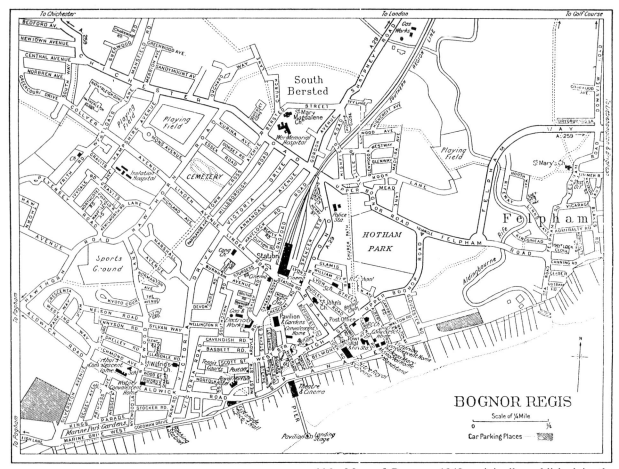

116 Map of Bognor, 1948, originally published in the *Town Guide*.

117 The south side of High Street in the 1950s. Osborne's and Leslie's cafés were popular spots for a 'cuppa'.

118 Christmas lights decorate the High Street in the 1950s.

119 Flooding in Belmont Street and York Road. Wade's the jewellers inhabited the north-west corner of the Kursaal building. Opposite was 'The Bijou' restaurant and Pennicott's, ladies outfitters (who later expanded to Aldwick Road premises).

120 In 1930 the Arcade caught fire and some of the damage is still visible in this view of Belmont Street. Wade's, a jeweller's on the right, is now replaced by the Regis Centre.

121 The foot of London Road, looking north, in 1921. Staley's on the corner was taken over by 'Bobby's' in the late 1950s.

122 A bustling London Road, *c*.1950, is dominated by the spire of St John's Church. Under the stone-carved letter 'P' on the right is Pink's, the grocers, tucked between Dutton & Thorowgood's shoe shop and Macfisheries. Other firm favourites in London Road were Lemmon's, a haberdashery shop which aimed to supply anything required, and Isted's, a corn merchant and grocer.

123 *(right)* Soldiers on parade (possibly following a service at St John's Church to give thanks for their safe return from France at the end of the First World War). In the background are International Stores, Colonial Stores and Mr. Hansford's shop. The latter site is now a gas showroom.

124 *(left)* The Rendezvous café in London Road—a meeting place no longer.

125 *(right)* Richmond Road, at the east side of the railway station.

126 John Street, 1969. This view was sent as a Christmas card from the occupants of no.18, with a printed note: 'Rescued, with others, by the Ministry of Housing and Local Government from an attempted Clearance Order by Bognor Regis Urban District Council'. Sadly, the cavalry did not get there in time twenty years later.

127 Queueing for meat outside Mant's, the pork butcher's in West Street, during the Second World War. The people are standing on the former site of the Pavilion, one of the first houses in Waterloo Square.

128 The bowling green in Waterloo Square, which opened in 1926.

129 Members of the Royal Observer Corps. standing on top of the old St John's Church tower in Market Street. This spot was used as a R.O.C. Observation Post *c.*1952-67. In the picture are, left to right: Mr. Mark Fairclough, Mr. Green, Mr. E.G. Brice, Mr. R. Harmer, Mr. H.A. Butt and Mr. L.G. Brice.

130 The promenade, west of the pier, *c*.1935.

131 The Esplanade Theatre, which started life as a horseshoe-shaped band enclosure in 1937, a roof not being added until 1947. Clive Dunn was just one of many entertainers who appeared here 'in their youth'. The theatre was demolished in 1980.

WEST END PROMENADE, BOGNOR REGIS 11701

132 An aerial view of west Bognor, *c.*1938, with the *Royal Norfolk Hotel*, the Rock Gardens and the Western Band Enclosure (later to be the Esplanade Theatre) all clearly visible.

133 This view of Bognor's sandy beach was taken in the 1930s, near the foot of Nyewood Lane. Note the beach huts, resting above a 10-ft. drop to the sands below—this gap has now been filled with shingle.

134 A well-known local fisherman, 'Dad' Allen, sitting amongst the prawn and lobster pots by Tamarisk Walk.

135 When the boat comes in ... Albert Ide, Billy Wellfare and Nelson Ide off-loading a catch of mackerel in the 1950s.

136 This seagull's view of Bognor, *c.*1938, clearly shows the 1902 pier pavilion and landing stage. During the 1950s divers launched themselves into the sea from here, entertaining holidaymakers with their daring routines. At that time, the pavilion housed a variety of penny amusements including a Kentucky Derby race. A miniature train, painted yellow and pink, cheerfully carried passengers up and down the length of the pier. Sadly, storms swept the pavilion away one night in March 1965. A collecting box for the 'Save the Pier Fund' was found lying on the sands the next day.

137 Built in 1908, the *Beaulieu Hotel* stood next door to the *Carlton Hotel* on Bognor's seafront.

138 The promenade near the foot of Nyewood Lane. The road was then named Goodman Drive but is now known as Marine Drive West.

139 Stocker Road, named after Dr. Stocker who owned the land until 1893. This site had once been used for horse-racing in the 1850s.

140 Aldwick Road, *c.*1930. The Broadway parade of shops on the right was built during the 1920s on the site of Mr. Edwin Thorp's vegetable plot.

141 After the storm: beach huts and the fishermen's sheds at Tamarisk Walk took a battering in 1967, leaving at least one local fisherman (Bryan Ide) to stand and stare.

142 Albie Ide making prawn pots, using withies, at the 'Pot Ranch'. This was an area belonging to local fishermen for the storage of their gear and was located at the foot of Gloucester Road. It is now a car park site.

Chapter Seven

'A Changing Identity'

The arrival of Butlin's at Bognor in 1960 was as significant as that of Sir Richard Hotham almost two hundred years earlier. The latter was probably turning in his grave as Bognor became nicknamed 'Butlin Regis'. Many local residents had very strong misgivings but the income generated from the lease was seen by the council as a means of achieving its ambitions for a grand new esplanade, free of fun-fairs and lined instead with impressive buildings.

In the town centre the Queensway development was under way, promising an exciting shopping experience. The West Meads housing estate was also springing up, described by a local journalist Gerard Young as a 'bungaloid disease'. The pier pavilion collapsed into the sea following storms and the sea even froze over during the winter of 1963.

During the early 1960s Bognor enjoyed a brief love affair with celluloid. Several feature films were produced here and the town's very own studio complex was optimistically planned.

Film actors Stanley Baker, Helmut Schmid and Tom Bell arrived in Bognor during February 1962. The local press excitedly reported Stanley Baker's arrival in his brand new bright-red 'E' type Jaguar, which must certainly have aroused local curiosity along Bognor's deserted wintry seafront. They were staying at the *Royal Hotel* whilst filming *A Prize of Arms*, a thriller about three ex-servicemen who plan a perfect crime—the theft of a quarter of a million pounds from a transit camp. Much of the location work was shot around Ford and Arundel, but one of the first scenes was set near the railway station, outside the newspaper depot in Richmond Road. At Ford Aerodrome, labourers from Bognor were employed to erect huts which were then promptly blown up for a film scene.

Just three months later and Bognor became 'Piltdown Bay' in the Tony Hancock film *The Punch and Judy Man*. Whilst staying at the *Royal Norfolk Hotel*, Hancock reminisced to local reporters about his early working days in Bognor. Back in 1949 he had been a member of the Flotsam's Follies playing to tiny audiences at the Esplanade Theatre, then a visible reminder from Hancock's hotel room. After Bognor came the radio series, then television, then his first film—*The Punch and Judy Man* was his second. An appeal was made to local residents to volunteer as film extras and over two thousand swarmed outside the *Royal Norfolk Hotel* in response.

The tale concerns a Punch and Judy man, contemptuous of the 'town hall lot' with which his snobby wife would dearly love to rub shoulders. After a disastrous performance at a civic dinner, held as part of the town's jubilee gala, when drunks wreck Hancock's act, his wife (played by Sylvia Syms) realises the folly of social climbing and she and Hancock leave the resort for a brighter future. Amongst the cast were John Le Mesurier, Mario Fabrizi, Hugh Lloyd and Barbara Murray.

Just months after the release of *The Punch and Judy Man* came news which really set Bognor buzzing. In December 1963 Sweethill Studios announced their intention of building on the Rookery Farm site studios to cater for international film making and television. On an area located between North Bersted Street and the South Bersted Industrial Estate plans were drafted for three large buildings, each 180-ft. long by 80-ft. wide and 40-ft. high, plus a three-storey administration block, a central power plant and storage facilities. After winning outline planning permission from the Chichester Rural Council, Sweethill Studios technical adviser, Mr. Victor Greene, outlined his own hopes for the future: 'I would suggest that the owners of existing studios who are facing these troubles [i.e. tight finances] should sell their land for housing and come and join us here, making a little Hollywood'.

However, Bognor was not destined to become a second Tinseltown. Mr. Greene was still optimistic in January 1965 but the Chichester Rural Council and West Sussex County Council, having discussed the matter every month since late 1963, declined to give Sweethill Studios the necessary go-ahead and Bognor was denied its chance of fame.

During the 1970s and early 1980s Bognor dipped into a trough of despair. The Kursaal, then known as the Rex Entertainment Centre, was demolished in 1975 and it left the morale of the town very low. There seemed no great improvement in fortune on the horizon. But as has so often been the case throughout the town's history, Bognor picked itself up and brushed itself off and is now revitalising its seafront. Time for another royal visit, perhaps?

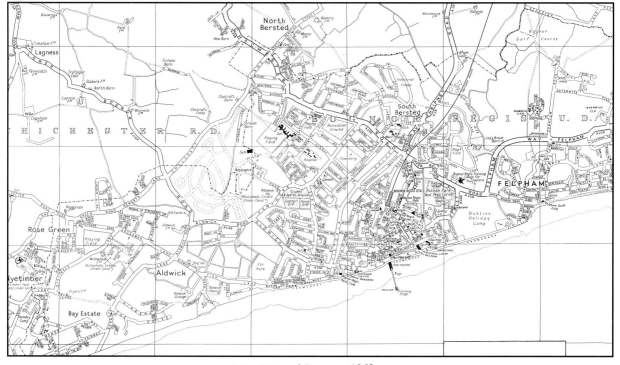

143 Map of Bognor, 1962.

144 High Street, early 1960s. The Southdown bus station on the left was built in 1934 and, despite its unique façade, was demolished sixty years later. Next door stands the Co-operative department store and neighbouring Cleeves (photographic suppliers). Beyond that, Bognor Motors.

145a Taken on 15 March 1960, this photograph shows the Queensway development after 3½ months' work by Bernard Sunley & Sons. Double-decker buses peer over the bus station wall next door (now Safeway's car park).

145b This photograph was taken on 22 March 1960, showing the foundations for Fitzleet House taking shape.

146a An aerial view, *c.*1947, of the Longbrook fields prior to their transformation into a Butlin's holiday camp. St Dominic's preparatory school had been demolished in the 1930s and that spot remained empty until Gloucester House was built in the 1960s.

146b The Butlin's camp, which opened in 1960, viewed across ornamental gardens lining the promenade.

147 The Boulevard caravan park, 1956. Many acres immediately north of Bognor were devoted to holiday caravan parks during the 1950s and 1960s. This particular site is now home to Tesco's.

148a Hotham Park House and the chapel clock. The chapel was built in the 1790s but demolished in 1859, leaving the clock to carry on counting time. It was restored in 1977 and continues to keep good time.

148b Pets Corner in Hotham Park, a popular children's attraction which opened in 1950. Now called Rainbow's End, it has been updated in line with today's trends and is still a great draw to children almost fifty years on.

148c At Pets Corner in Hotham Park, Minnie Mouse sat beside an invitingly empty chair. Many a family snapshot must have been taken here!

149 The white flour mill, by the shore at Felpham—at 4 p.m., 18 February 1879, to be precise! Chas. Lewis, an engraver by trade, drew this sketch as the mill was being demolished. Mr. Lewis lived at Cavendish Villa, Felpham Road, and died the following year, 1880, at the age of seventy-three. He is buried at Felpham church, opposite the porch.

150 The 'Old Mill', Snooks Corner, Felpham, which was built on the former site of the black mill (used for grinding flour)

151 The centre of Felpham village, *c.*1900. Felpham is mentioned in Domesday Book; the church at the heart of the village is Norman, but is believed to have Saxon origins. More unlikely is the claim that Felpham was the spot where the last transaction of a man selling his wife took place.

152 The post office at Felpham, *c.*1905. Note the car and the policeman keeping a wary eye on it.

153a *The Fox* pub in Vicarage Lane, Felpham catches fire in October 1946.

153b The thatched roof of the saloon bar also catches alight.

153c Afterwards, villagers inspect the considerable damage. The new *Fox* reopened in January 1950.

154 Blakes Road, Felpham. In the distance (on the right) stands Blake's Cottage, named after the poet William Blake who lived here between 1800 and 1803.

155 Felpham beach, 1920s.

156 Felpham Way, with the old school (opened in 1888) standing on the left. There were neither congestion nor traffic lights in the 1930s.

157 The *Brewer's Arms* on Felpham Way, *c.*1910. Said to have dated from the 18th century, this inn was demolished in the 1920s and the present *Southdowns Hotel* was built almost next door.

158 Middleton old church in 1795, lost to the encroaching sea in the late 1830s.

159 'The New City', a pioneer holiday camp which opened in 1922 on the former site of the Norman Thompson Flight Company at Middleton. The hotel comprised 200 bedrooms and the New City even had its own dairy and farm, as well as electrical plant for lighting and heating.

160a The Norman Thompson Flight Company, which began construction of aircraft at Middleton in 1910, specialising in seaplanes. During the First World War orders flowed in from the Royal Naval Air Service—the factory supplied 50 of their twin-engined flying-boats for U-boat patrols in the North Sea. Business slumped after the War and the company folded in 1919.

160b A staff photograph taken during the busy years at the Norman Thompson Flight Company. This picture was loaned by Mrs. D. Glue, who is in the second row from the top.

161 The beach at Elmer in the 1920s.

162 Main Road, Elmer.

MAIN ROAD, ELMER 6

163 *(above)* Aldwick village in the 1930s.

164a *(above right)* Margaret House, near Aldwick duckpond, in 1954. In 1932 Sir Roland Rank rented the house to Barnardo's and then bequeathed it to the charity in 1939. For over thirty years Margaret House was home to 35 boys at any one time. Now demolished, Margaret Close occupies the site.

164b *(right)* Sir Roland Rank treats the Barnardo's boys to an 'Antarctic' ice-cream on Bognor beach in 1936.

165 Martineau House, a seaside school for disadvantaged children from 1955 until its demolition in 1995. The house was previously known as Craigweil Lodge and was home to the Stocker family for many years.

166 Craigweil House was built in the 18th century by the Countess of Newburgh. In 1915 Sir Arthur du Cros bought it and enlarged the house. King George V spent two months convalescing here in 1929, during which time a Privy Council was held at Craigweil House when the King dissolved Parliament. The house was demolished in 1939.

167a The Bay Estate, Aldwick. This 'new seaside garden city' began life in the late 1920s.

167b The Tithe Barn Club on the Aldwick Bay Estate, which opened in September 1932. Damaged by fire in the summer of 1954, it was not until March 1960 that the club could be re-opened by Ruby Miller. By 1972 plans were afoot to replace the Tithe Barn with flats—which did indeed happen.

168a Paradise Cottage at Aldwick. Built *c.*1802, just west of Dark Lane, it was the indulgence of Sir Thomas Brooke Pechell and he called it Aldwick Villa. Honeysuckle and jasmine entwined decorative pillars lining the verandah. Sir Thomas's son, George, was M.P. for Brighton for 25 years and equerry to Queen Adelaide.

168b Rev. Croxton Johnson was the last owner of 'Paradise'. He built a chapel for fishermen in the house grounds, but when the chapel was later converted into a residence (and the organ removed to Bognor's Masonic Hall), the ghost of a sailor was seen in the house.

168c In April 1909 fire swept through 'Paradise' and only smouldering walls and charred chimneys remained. The Rev. Croxton Johnson's daughter-in-law continued to live there, in what is now the converted chapel, until her death in 1929.

169 Early settlers at Pagham beach!